PISTACHIOS
in my Pocket

PISTACHIOS
in my Pocket

SAREH
FARMAND

AT BAY
press

WINNIPEG

Pistachios in my Pocket

Design and layout by Matthew Stevens and M. C. Joudrey.

Published by At Bay Press October 2022.

Library and Archives Canada cataloguing in publication is available upon request.

ISBN 978-1-988168-69-2

Printed and bound in Canada.

This book is printed on acid free paper that is 100% recycled ancient forest friendly (100% post-consumer recycled).

This book was made with the generous support of the Manitoba Arts Council and the Canada Council for the Arts.

First Edition

10 9 8 7 6 5 4 3 2 1

atbaypress.com

For my family.

CONTENTS

Preface

When the Islamic Republic took over Iran, my family was unhomed.

Just two years before, in 1976, my parents were wed and blissfully unaware of what was ahead, as they embarked on a new life together with boundless hope for their future. They had no reason to believe that their plans would cease to exist, and that their lives would be turned upside down.

With broken hearts and endless concerns over facing the uncertainties of immigration, my family fled to Canada via Berlin and Rome. They left behind everything they knew, and everyone they loved in a homeland amid great change.

The story of humanity itself is that of leaving one's home and community, to create another elsewhere, and my parents' lives are now another thread woven into that story. They fled with only their memories, hopes, and me: a three-year-old girl in a proper coat with pistachios in her pocket.

For context, the Iranian Revolution began in the early 70s with university educated youth wanting greater equality. Many believed Iran's socio-political structure was too elitist with a hierarchical system running on nepotism and ruled by a greedy monarchy and elite upper class. However, what began as a movement for greater equality and a call for democracy was hijacked by Ayatollah Khomeini, President Carter[1], and the British Government[2] (see poem CIA, M16). As a result, a conservative far-right theocracy filled the void of the falling monarchy. 1978, the year I was born and a clandestine year for Iran, marks the beginning of the modern Dark Ages under an Islamic fundamentalist government called the Islamic Republic of Iran.

The Iranian Revolution impacted people differently. Many people, such as my family, fled Iran because under the new regime they were persecuted for their political beliefs, religion, and class.

In my experience, no beauty or ingenuity has ever come from the government of the Islamic Republic of Iran and its supporters. Every glorious act of discovery and expression achieved by any Iranian within or outside of Iran has been accomplished in spite of them—like the book you hold in your hand.

These poems are the stories and experiences I have collected along the way in building our new home in Canada. It is about similarities, differences, and struggles to fit in. It is about welcoming, multiculturalism, safety, and fear. Fleeing and losing. Finding and creating.

---

[1] Hamid Dabashi, Iran: A People Interrupted (New York: The New Press, 2008), 145-147.

[2] Mark Curtis, "Britain and the Iranian Revolution: Expediency, Arms, and Secret Deals", February 1 2019, https://www.middleeasteye.net/opinion/britain-and-iranian-revolution-expediency-arms-and-secret-deals

Desert Sky

revolution

chaos raises me

upheaves   the sides of the ancient rug my family bestows upon me

birds of paradise ravage lotus flowers
blood stains cypress trees
dissidents hang from the tree of life
        dad diverts my gaze:
                a gazelle leaps across the haze

morning in Tehran

marmalade light
       slowly fills the slate streets

air crisp
clean
arid

city
stirs from slumber
sits in quiet prayer upon
          rectangle
          silk
          carpets

paisley pinks and blues   soft   beneath clean morning feet

sapphire

under sapphire skies   spotted with stars
Maryam[3] climbs the rooftop of her parent's one storey house
awaiting the euphony
of businessmen coming home on camelback trade expeditions

her father and uncles ride gentle golden beasts   to foreign lands
and back again
before King Reza Shah Pahlavi decrees mandatory motorization·

    a musical procession   she can hear from afar
breaking silence
growing louder   families crowd quietly on rooftop verandas
listening

  camels adorned with wares from the marketplace
around their necks and bodies
clink clank   clink clank   clink clank in tempo to
their tough   tired hoofs as percussion to
 whistling from fathers
  poetry recited by uncles
sing-song echoes from sons
                        returning home

---

[3] My maternal grandmother.

Maryam

runs through meadows
beats all the boys in races
scolded for not acting lady like

    climbs trees
        darn skirt always
  gets in the way

finishes school
raises three children, widowed
        never
        losing
        the gleam
            in her amber almond eyes

horses[4]

I don't like riding horses, but I never tell my granddaughters

I was nine years old the first time I rode a horse
I wasn't interested in riding a horse until a pinch-faced boy and his
proper father told me horseback riding was not for girls
at that moment, my interest grew acute
 this I tell my granddaughters

the father's words, a spring, I use to jump on the broad brown beast
next to him
I pull up the hem of my long crepe skirt, grab hold of the harness
around its neck
throw my legs on either side of its back, feel the barrel of its body
on my calves
 I look down at father and son
they are dumbfounded, the father worriedly puts a hand on the
harness
the horse moves a little, I teeter
he laughs, I clutch the horse with my legs
he says *okay, you have proven your point, now get down*
his words build fire

my granddaughters love this part of the story

I grip my heels— the horse takes off, fast
I hold onto the harness strong, clamp my legs harder and harder

---

[4] As told by my maternal grandmother, Maryam.

not to fall, this makes the horse go faster and faster— I gallop
across the father's field, whizz by my family so fast I barely hear my
mother yell: *Khodayah, Maryam*! Bushes, trees, and shrub whirl
by— I am terrified
but I keep going, I cannot stop, I don't know how—
will I go to the ends of the earth like this?

I yank back hard on the harness.
The horse slows to a stop. I lurch back, forth, and finally settle.
I catch my breath
 my skirt catches my tears
 hands and harness are one
I deepen my breath
 my heartbeat slows
 my shoulder blades glide down my back
I manage to turn the horse around by nudging its head to the side
over and over
I gingerly push my legs into his body to make him move, I figured
this out!

I trot back along the chip rock road

history of the veil

The history of the veil in Iran mirrors the history of women's rights and freedoms. The struggle between the religious right and the State for control over the nation is as old as Iran itself, and with it the policies of veiling and the status of women's rights and freedoms.

My maternal grandmother experienced the first legal unveiling of women in Iran, which to her more liberal family, was a welcome change.

Veiling was brought to Iran in 633 AD with the Arab-Islamic invasion when women were mandated to wear the traditional "chador" (a large piece of cloth) to cover their head and body or the "hijab" (a head-scarf) to cover their head, ears, and neck, and a "manteau" (a knee length jacket) covering their body. Over the centuries, women's clothing evolved in various forms under various monarchies; however, in Iran, there has never been a policy to cover women's faces.

In 1936, Reza Shah Pahlavi outlawed wearing the hijab and chador as part of his plan for secularization and modernization. Throughout the Pahlavi era great strides were made with women's rights that placed the status of women akin to the status of women in Western countries.

In the early 1970s, women protesting the monarchy and wanting a democratically elected parliamentary system wore the hijab as a symbol to protest the Shah, the monarchy, and western feminism, which they felt was not true feminism.

In 1979, the Islamic Republic of Iran enforced a strict Islamic dress code for all women, which meant veiling.

On March 8th, 1979, more than 100,000 women gathered on the streets of Tehran to protest the new Islamic government's compulsory hijab ruling. To this day, women in Iran are forced to veil, regardless of their religious beliefs.

unveiling[5]

I

home
warmed   by the smell of saffron

father's newspaper rustles

mother's prayer beads
        slide-tap
slide-tap
        slide-tap
                as she murmurs prayers
                in her rocking chair

I am hunched over the Russian rosewood coffee table
from one of Father's trade expeditions
studying

my sisters taunt
why do you study so hard? you won't need all that once you're married.
they don't understand

II

my sister Marzieh and I walk to school
early winter cools the air

_____

[5] In Maryam's voice.

wool berets to the side of our heads
 mine navy, not black
you always have to be different, mother scoffs
 same is so boring

behind me sudden thumping horse hooves
screeching whistles twisting my head
I see
police on horseback pluck the headscarves off two classmates
and gallop away

shrieks fill the air
books tumble to the ground
arms coil around heads
tears cascade   sisters stammer around each other
run home

I turn and run toward them   nab their books off the dusty road
chase
I've always been a fast runner— beat all the boys
my legs lead me ahead of the girls
I whip around to stop them: wait!
why are you crying? you won't get in trouble—the law's been changed

the chador is our religious right
you don't understand

mullah

mosques brimming with morning disciples in sunrise prayers

my family at home making tea
my aunt plays her Beatles record while my mother is scorned for
wanting to attend mosque
> *it's too political a place*
> *you don't need a mullah to lead you to God*
> *You are a child of the universe*
> *Khoda means God within self*
> *search within yourself for the answers*

later, sisters walk to school, hand in hand
my mom's gaze traces
> horseshoe arches
> > pillars of brickwork
> > > tall minaret

mullahs stare back, thumbing their prayer beads beneath their
shawls
plotting away her freedom, one bead at a time
simply counting the days

mini-jupe[6]

        we had

wide open spaces   desert wind blowing our hair

        we had

carefree laughter, cheer
British invasion mixed with Persian heritage
shy, I wore my mini skirt to the outdoor ice cream parlour
scent of rosewater filling the air

           your new haircut makes you look like Ringo Starr, he yelled
           my cousin gave him a good look
           at her homemade manicured middle finger

           we laughed in his stupid face
           she let his surprise linger

        we had

light breezes upon the garden fountain
           ancient turquoise blue
           hand-painted tiles
           artwork artifacts   beneath the surface of the water

---

[6] In the voice of my mother in her late teens. Mini-jupe means mini skirt in French and in Farsi. France tried to colonize Iran for many years.

then, a shot in the rain
and nothing was the same

    they had
        guns pointing at their friends
        neighbours giving names, lest they be blamed
        angry political street chants
        batons, pepper spray

I wore my miniskirt to the dance

vacay

socks off   pale skin   black bikini

red toenails gleam   in white sand

blue grey waves   of the Caspian Sea roar

drown out anguished city streets

politics melt off
                    mom's
                              young feet

discordant

dutiful players on a chess board
clearly defined
black and white

you both meet every expectation   beautifully

humble yet successful
hardworking
helpful
save your money, pay in cash, enjoy life, but don't be lavish
judgement leaves no room for error
prizes awarded later

abruptly an illegitimate player enters
commissioned by England and the US
swings his bony, wrinkly, liver-spotted, thieving hand
   scatters pieces
               chaos

deceptions

audience desperate to believe   we latch onto every syllable
hidden anchors in each word   placed to drown us

the physics of power: we fall   they rise

God watches children play
as soldiers surround the park

caviar [7]

was it the last time I saw you?

we have the good caviar
crackers crumble in the seam of the porcelain plate
sapphire pebbles on iridescent spoons

tension tugs   silent air

so far away from where we began
negate telling me   anything at all
deciding to leave Tehran, for what?

then again, you always were the child who got away

[7] In the voice of my paternal grandmother.

CIA, M16

my paternal grandmother could not let go of her satin-silk ideas of Iran
the unravelled weft of her skirt held tightly in her fist
fraying material losing connective tissue
 peacock-coloured strings
                falling
      through the air
                      in piles upon her pink shoes

she hears raucous noise below her east facing balcony where she loves
to watch the sunrise spill its cocktail colours
on her carefully placed possessions

> *The CIA has released documents which for the first time
> formally acknowledge its key role in the 1953 coup, which
> ousted Iran's democratically elected Prime Minister,
> Mohammad Mosaddeq. [BBC News, 20 August 2013]*

turquoise blue skies were the backdrop to her jagged mountain views
each crown tip frosted by snow

> *This is believed to be the first time the CIA has itself
> admitted the part it played in concert with the British
> intelligence agency, M16. The documents were published in
> the independent National Security Archive on the 60th
> anniversary of the coup. [BBC News, 20 August 2013]*

my maternal grandmother could not hide her Audrey Hepburn elegance
 despite dressing like the rebels:
black cloaks, by choice
to distinguish them from
American barbie doll feminists   and Iranian imperialists

Iran's epiphany for equal rights and democracy   hijacked

> *The clerical class had been on the defensive ever since the 1920s when the secular anti-clerical Reza Shah Pahlavi became King of Iran. Reza's son, Mohammad Reza Shah, instituted a "White Revolution" which the Ulama (religious scholars) disliked as it called for land reform, nationalization of forests, enfranchisement of women, non-Muslims to hold office, and a literacy campaign in the nation's schools. These initiatives were regarded as dangerous Westernizing trends by the Ulama and Khomeini viewed them as "an attack on Islam". Ayatollah Khomeini led a boycott of the referendum on the White Revolution in 1963 and as a result was exiled in 1964. (Adib-Moghaddam, Arshin. A Critical Introduction to Khomeini. Cambridge: Cambridge University Press, 2015)*

my mother in her living room
the only living room that is ever
truly hers
friends are there, she is safe
in this unknown time, coffee dates turn to dinner parties
there is safety in numbers
  there is safety indoors

when it is time to go home, there are riots on the streets
so you overstay, are welcome

> *Documents seen by BBC suggest the Carter administration*
> *paved the way for Khomeini to return to Iran in 1978 by*
> *holding the army back from launching a military coup. [The*
> *Guardian, Fri 10 Jun 2016]*

the cold silk of the hand knotted rug rests at the soles of their shoes
as they criss-cross, criss-cross, criss-cross their legs

Turkish coffee has been savoured
its sweet-musky smell lingers
small cups are overturned onto saucers   awaiting prophecy
 in uncertain times

> *Khomeini's message is part of a trove of newly declassified*
> *US government documents … that tell the largely unknown*
> *story of America's secret engagement with Khomeini … This*
> *story is a detailed account of how Khomeini brokered his*
> *return to Iran using a tone of deference and amenabil-*
> *ity towards the US that … neither government has ever*
> *admitted. Far from defying America, the ayatollah courted*
> *the Carter administration … portraying a potential Islamic*
> *Republic as amenable to US interests. (BBC News, June 3,*
> *2016)*

an axis is built   East-West
we must choose   one or the other

changes

transfixed
  in one moment
   nothing remains the same

and I am alright
 I am alright
  all right with change

but we have quiet longing
for our past
pulling at our core

         warming milk on open fires
         raising tents out in the sky
         playing under sheets
         while daylight passes us by
         safer than in heaven
         when no one knows our name

while we are daylight dreaming
enmity breeds

rose petals

kettles hiss
inside every home
spluttering hot water on cold tile floors

toaster ovens tick tick tick tick
warm *sangak* bread

grandma takes a silver spoon
of Persian tea leaves to her favourite teapot
stained on the inside, deep sienna, from years of use
the colour of Persian soil

an earthy aroma of black tea leaves, dried rose petals, and carda-
mom laces the air
she breathes it in as she drowns the tea leaves in a pool of shallow
boiling water
setting it on the opening of the gold-plated *samovar*

later in the day, the tea leaves will be read:
> *change is on the way: great upheaval*
what could it be, they wonder
> *the leaves say: a baby, big change, great upheaval*
they linger on the baby, I am a glimmer

years later, her favourite teapot had to stay back
the big change, the great upheaval did not let her

take comforts of her old life
she searches now to find them

down grocery aisles: familiar ingredients
in antique shops: her silverware and tea-set
along sidewalks: an old neighbour or co-worker?
in flea markets: her favourite teapot

pennyroyal flower

far inside the city
revolution rages
divisive voices
 conflicting ideologies
fighting for freedom

         who's fighting?
         whose freedom?

our serene suburb
Mama Maryam and I inside our kitchen
hot outside air threatens the air conditioner
 soft battle at the open side door

grandma sings off-tune

    La la la la Goleh Pooneh
    Geddah oomad dareh khooneh[8]

I soak it up like honey milk to sweet bread
she giggles while she sings aware she is off key

suddenly her face changes
I see someone peering in from our side door
kneeling
dirty
toothless grin
an old beggar

---

[8] Goleh Pooneh is an old Iranian lullaby that is about a beggar coming to someone's home and begging for food and shelter. The line above translates as: La la la la pennyroyal flower/the beggar has come to the front door.

asking us for something
rapid back and forth
my grandma flustered leaves the room
fetching the woman what she wants

the toothless lady smiles at me
out from under her shawl
bony arms crinkly skin wave at me

in plain view my fat legs
dangle in my highchair
plum pudding drips from my spoon

veiling: the personal is political[9], 1979

I

burgundy and brass, busy office

sunburst clock upon wood panel wall

scent of coffee, rose-water pistachio cookies, cool climatized air

my mother's shoes   echo in hallways of cold white porcelain tile
drown quiet on wine-coloured carpets

since the revolution, everyone is tense, even here

she hurriedly slides open her desk drawer
puts away her purse   not noticing
the framed picture of the Shah
on the wall behind her desk   is missing

she enters the terse energy of the meeting room   everyone is told

mandatory veiling for all female personnel begins tomorrow

lips tighten
eyes widen
heads shake from side to side
bodies shudder

---

[9] Coined in 1968 by Carol Hanisch, a civil rights and feminist activist. In the voice of my mother.

hands tremble

knees knock

female personnel look at one another

  others look away

some of these women might agree with this absurdity, she reminds

herself

we are not all the same

sees

      rage

in the eyes of her friends

             rage

for an extremist regime legitimized by the people

they wanted change, is this the type of change they had in mind?

she screams

inside herself

her body stiffens

too scared to speak   a shroud of silence fills the room

II

I left work early on that cursed day. When I woke up, I never
imagined this would have been my last day at the office. After the
ridiculous meeting, where my supervisor could not even look us in
the eye, we took a long coffee break. Not everyone of course, but
Shahpar, Jila, Zahra, and I did. We could hardly speak- what can
you say when your freedom and rights are being stripped away in
your own country? Your homeland that promised you safety, upward

mobility, freedom?

I took my purse and said goodbye to my supervisor who looked
like he had been crying. He too was mad, embarrassed, and in fear
of what else this regime might do. That was our last encounter.
With mutual respect and sinking hearts, we parted.

I walked home and it took me forever.
I am not sure if I ever arrived.
Not sure if I have arrived there still.

mom's handwriting

in the midst of turmoil, we continue
  turn bomb threats into midnight basement parties
  turn ayatollah chants into childhood games:
  when we hear them on the street say, I am the leader!

little do we know what will be

a silver kitchen radio tells mom diapers have arrived at the store
after fitting them on shelves in our hallway closet, my uncle calls:
        a car will pick you up tomorrow and take you out
        you can return when this whole thing blows over
        you need to get out, while you still can

frozen cold in the stifling warm home
staring at the wall of diapers
mom responds, but I am so well-prepared

          - bill payment due dates written on the kitchen calendar
          - in a year, I'll ask for a promotion at work
          - we'll have four kids
          - school lunch kotlet and kabob leftovers
          - big family picnics at Park-E-Prince
          - Saturday morning visits where my father is laid to rest
          - our old friends, like family
          - plans for the garage extension

- Norooz[10] in Iran
- my land
- my home
- my land
- …

the grocery list in mom's handwriting
tucked in a corner of the kitchen under the lower cabinets
unseen in the empty house
on yellowing linoleum

---

[10] The first day of the Iranian new year occurring on the vernal equinox.

glass[11]

I

I dreamt I asked my grandmother
to laugh in a glass jar
so I could carry her laughter away with me from place to place

if only I had

we escaped
through silent snow fields
  fled as darkness grew thick through a path my father paid to
memorize
  (prayed was still safe)

I wonder if Maman could hear three heartbeats
 the baby she carried   the mother she left behind her own

II

I was never like the women of Iran
a Russian-Christian amongst Iranian-Muslims
but always welcome

I wore Russian fashions
heavy shawls

---

[11] The narrator in this poem is my maternal great-great-grandmother who fled from Russia to Iran during the Bolshevik revolution with her family.

crimson   umber   turquoise   canary-yellow   wool thread
my granddaughters, Maryam and Marzieh
hiding between the pleats of my long skirts
falling asleep on my shawls
hiding my shoes so I could not leave their home after visits

living
the life my father dared us to dream

III

one day
from far above
on my whipping cream cloud
I watched it unfold

through thick black smoke, deep into angry chants
  Maryam and Marzieh fleeing Iran
  wishing they had the sound of their grandmother's laughter
in a glass jar

mix tape[12]

my parents, stressed, in the car
for weeks they had planned our leaving
it was scary leaving Iran, all my family, my friends, my school, my
house

but neighbours across the street were taken by Islamic
fundamentalists
the men who took them had beards and wild hair
I saw them swerve in front of the house across the street
I saw the whole thing
they had guns
they were yelling
one guy looked at me
I looked back
our eyes momentarily locked
I held my little cousin tighter in my arms

maybe that could happen to us if we stay

my parents and brother are in the car, impatient
I tell them I forgot something and run back inside, without
permission
my parents yell after me to stop
but I have to
I have to
I have to get mom's favourite tapes, she forgot to pack them

---

[12] Told in my cousin's ten year old voice.

she will miss them terribly

I am back inside my home
the warmth, the smell, the security envelops me like a blanket
I quickly go to the stereo and grab her favourite tapes

once we are in Rome, I give them to her
she cries
holds me

she plays them all the time

God's country

dawn broke the desert sky
we crossed the border into new territory

in my ribcage
        all night
        I was holding
        the dreaded anticipation of the border-guard exchange
with my parents
        everyone could feel it, in their lungs, on their chest, its
tight grip on the flow of oxygen in the clenched corners of the
Volkswagen bus
        a vise
muffled words, tension at the state line, we feigned an air of
comfort, suffocated in fear

hiding pearl white earrings in pistachio shells, you turned to me
pretending you were not crying   we crossed
                          into safety
                          breathing

your grief now had room in my ribcage
I held it
        with you
        from you
        for you
        give me all of it, if only my two-year old body was not so small

looking for answers, I asked the peach-skin sun

will we ever be back home?

dad's laughter rolled with his tears
let's pretend this is not the end

New Moon

unhomed

I woke up from my dream
in the old house by the stairs
it was dusty   we were pale
after years of no one there

every nook   every cranny
had trace DNA
evidence of you and me
evidence we were once free

who took over the lives meant for us
our possessions their prize

politician-mullahs emboldened
ideals held tightly in their breath
smoked softly through their chest
people took to streets   fighting for peace
whose peace were they seeking

Iran stolen

now we miss
the heat
orange blossoms in rain
live this daisy chain diaspora   our ears perked for mother language

river

 time of in-between
could be liberating
instead confining
  unable to move forward
the present, stifling

parents plan picnics beside the Tiber River
where the plump green moss is well-hydrated by our tears

 time of in-between
daydreaming under cloudless skies
endless possibilities
 where will we be someday could be liberating
        chanting, greedy mullahs
        rage on
        hijack safety

the life my parents planned
sketched in their heads
pinned to vision boards
now stripped
needs a new blueprint

at night, we lie side-by-side on roll out mats
in rental apartments for immigrants and refugees
listening to each other breathe

soft

baseboard heaters
　　　　tick tick tick　　grinding gears
　　　　　　　　　　　　low and rumbling
in the　for-now-home

you
the lifeline
 the ones we knew back home
 the home where the heart is

everything unfamiliar
language, streets, social norms, noise, currency, climate, food, faces,
places—

you
family, old friends, colleagues, once neighbours
comfort in chaos
you
softness on this new map of sharply shattered dreams

snow

warm amber light embrace
home filled with family
kitchen clean-up sounds
percussion to our laughter

two little girls hurriedly dressed
thick warm snowsuits   puffy mittens   scratchy wool scarves and
hats
cover everything
  except round cheeks   button nose   our eyes
mine brown, hers blue

led outside
bright white and grey

muffled quiet
small snow-filled landing
stairs ahead, we are told not to climb
cold air enters soft noses
warm lungs
door closes

hush fills the air

smiles and looks hide language barriers

she shows me to slosh wet white snow with my mittens
manoeuvre it like playdough

        slish   slosh   slish slosh   slish slosh   slosh slosh

I pat-pat-pat my little snow mound
watch for her approval
smiling at my blob

she has built a snow-white crystal castle

Berlin, 1980

trying to mend this broken dream with raffia is exhausting
but that is all they seem to have at their German night markets

adorning our rental apartment with pale blue flowers
picked along school yard fences
I find eyelet ribbon to make a bow
burn vanilla candles to mask the smell of cat pee

an open smile to neighbouring strangers
should at least scratch
their cold-climate ice-thick stares
but little do they want to do with us

this rental has an eerie light
casts distant memories
shadows dance
where past-present unite
on the open floor

I make my tea and steep it
boiling water into me
I watch the seasons stumble
wonder one day where we'll be

Rome, 1981

we walk
 through starlit streets of Rome
navy velvet air holding us

those lucky Romans
home is still their home
 land their father
   language their mother tongue
     under their grandparents' sky

-not at the mercy of consulate red rubber stamps-

our footsteps
        break silence

bounce off
        terra cotta tile balconies
dad whistles
       it echoes back
sing, he says

my voice spills
 onto streets
    carries over homes
      past railway lines
       ripples along rivers

climbs mountains

carves canyons

longs Iran

my voice echoes

in empty rooms

subdues upon sunken chairs

traces framed family photos

water-stained baseboards

climbs into my empty crib

so lonely without a home

motherland

you are here
      all around
           yet you are gone

          no body   only shadows
          no soil   only dusted memories
    nothing to touch   I trace your outline on glossy picture paper

               doorway arches
               mountain curves
               winding roads
               to nowhere

you are held in the corners of my mind
        tight crevasses of my heart
        you line my lungs
        and gut with microbes
        found only in your geography
everything that makes me strong is born from you

so far away
I live and breathe you still
I use your love language to whisper sweetness in my babies' ears
 savoury scent of your food fills our Canadian home
your old songs, I know by heart

you
gone
 yet forever remain
within   around me

harbouring hope[13]

June 28th 1981
we are still
living in Rome

harbouring hope
the Revolution will blow over
we will go back
lead normal lives

one day, people will make great art, write in-depth sociopolitical
articles
add pages to the history books about
that crazy time in the 70s when the mullahs almost took over Iran

we are optimists

I will myself to hold onto a vision:
her little hand in mine, walking into our home
sighing relief as she runs to find her toys

do they call this denial?

there is a moment

      June 28th 1981— Hafte Tir[14]
      Tehran, Iran— Headquarters

---

[13] This poem is told in my father's voice.
[14] Hafte Tir signifies the date June 28th as it translates in the Iranian calendar as the 7th day of the month of Tir: 7 tir 1360.

of the newly established
Islamic Republic Party—
during a meeting with high-rank-
ing party leaders a bomb
explodes— kills 73 leading offi-
cials of the Islamic Republic Party.
Kills Chief Justice Ayatollah
Mohammad Beheshti, the second
most powerful figure in the
Revolution

does this mean what we hope?

the Revolution this nightmare
finally over
Iran is being freed
trepidatious exhilaration

we say to one another
I told you so, I knew this would not last
God heard our prayers, listened to true believers

only to discover

June 30th 1981— Rome, Italy— International
news sources reporting— the 73 leading offi-
cials were killed by hardliners,
to make room for the extremists.

others have God's ear
ugly truth emerges
there is no
going back
home

Sepi braiding my hair

under
drizzle of rain
parasol pine trees line the Aniene river
children hold hands
collect rocks
whisper new songs in
soft ears

my friend Sepi is older than me
she bridges the pre-teen kids and me, the youngest
she stops, on the path so I stop too
she begins to braid my hair, I love it when she does this
mom never braids my hair anymore

adults speak emphatically
pass us by

*We have friends who took to the streets for equality between the classes
which was a valid reason. Don't you think? My own mother wore the
chador in opposition to Western feminism! I mean, I agree that U.S.
feminism's sexualized woman is a farce, not feminism; but look where
the fight got us. Well, that's because the movement was hijacked by the
far right, England, and the US.*

I close my eyes to the softness of Sepi braiding my hair

under
parasol pine trees lining the Aniene river
mothers and fathers
family and friends
collect new memories
whisper old dreams
tumultuous times together

I open my eyes
see the women link arms
safe
under parasol pines

they knock

there is a small place
a space in your head
where spirits can roam
undisturbed

they find the path through your spine and slowly walk up the curve
they knock three times at the base of your skull where the light
shines and pools
they enter there, find peace from snares, take off their dusty shoes

they visit me, these spritely beings, and keep me amused
so earthly things, shattered dreams, stay in the adult room

wish

dad, I see the outline of cypress trees tall in your eyes

mom, you cry when you tell me about Persian soil:
Khakeh-Iran-e-ma[15]

(on your birthdays, I long to take you home   make you truly
happy again)

---

[15] This phrase translates to "our Persian soil" and it is a line directly from the national anthem (not the current Islamic Fundamentalist anthem) under the Shah.

leave, again[16]

tagging luggage on a muggy day in Rome
air conditioner struggles

heart wrenching cries   two boys surrender their sorrows   at the
international gate
chilling everyone frozen

immense grief cannot fit in small bodies

I don't understand their language
but know broken hearts

they clench onto an older woman, perhaps their Grandmother,
afraid to let her go
their parents beg them to stop, *please just come nicely!*

the children grip the woman's fingers, hands, elbows, shoulders
pull her arms, purse, sweater
curl into her tear-drenched neck, shoulders
grasp her waist with their arms
bury their heads in her stomach
clasp her knees, ankles, shoes
 cry so many tears we could all be washed clean

she sobs shaking tries to keep herself steady
comforts and kisses

---

[16] Told from the perspective of an airline attendant on the day my cousins left Rome to immigrate to Canada in 1980.

cradles their faces in her trembling hands

I will see you one day again, but the children need greater assurance
she can barely speak

the father struggles to be firm, just stop this nonsense
the mother pulls herself together long enough to say, *stop this now,*
you are making a scene
their children's suffering shatters resilience

we are all helpless   suspended in grief
God help them

diaphanous

lightly stitched we are

with heavy hands   thick knuckles   thin skin

we are lightly stitched
together

we tenderize small wounds
on calloused walls
of our heart chambers

defining

Home

- where one lives
- or has lived
- for some time

- where one lives
- or has lived
- over a period of time as a member of a family or household

- place that informs and permeates our thoughts
- follows us
- no matter how far

diaspora

I

Berlin,
where we find respite
where Iranians don't require travel visas, just yet
reprieve

> *things will get better, they say*
> *the revolution will die down*
> *the Shah will be back*
> *Iran will have a constitutional monarchy,* they hope

children play by fireplaces and outside in snow
        adults set tables with white eyelet tablecloths
we learn German nursery rhymes
        our parents learn to roast duck and goose
everyone enjoys kaffe-kuchen[17]

II

in a dark corner
on a small lacquered table
my mom sets up a black RCA tape recorder

this is what you speak into, her instructions always cloaked in warm
love

---

[17] This phrase translates literally to "coffee and cake" but refers to the ritual of a leisurely gathering with friends or family for a chat over some cake and coffee.

I sit
on my little red wooden chair and we record our voices
I giggle with glee, playing this game with my mom
playing back our voices, we love each other, I can hear it

because of the revolution we sing songs   say messages
into the tape deck for our family and friends
all over the world

I play the tapes back until the day they are mailed off
somewhere far away   Sydney, LA, Vienna, Rome, Vancouver,
Tehran…

nobody sends one back   or maybe they do   but we have already
moved

III

Rome,
you are not giving landed immigrant applications to Iranians
a web of family
and friends
hold us safe
temporary, here

things will get better, they say
the revolution will die down
the Shah will be back
Iran will have a constitutional monarchy, they repeat

my cousins attend international school with Iranian kids we know
I stay home wishing I was old enough
weekends are for picnics under balboa trees
branches sway above our blankets
 leaves like stained glass against light
we feast on succulent Roman olives, sun-kissed tomatoes, and sharp
Lebanese feta
  requiring this Roman Holiday

mom sets up the RCA tape recorder
this time on an empty wooden wine crate
turned upside down on terra cotta tiles of the dining room

I sit on cushions, face the balcony and record my voice
into the tape deck for our family and friends
all over the world

I play the tapes back
until they are mailed off
 somewhere far away
  nobody sends one back   or maybe they do   but we are already gone

Northern Lights

North Vancouver, 1982

in my pink raincoat
from Mrs. Müeller's shop on Lonsdale
where we always speak our German   so Mrs. Müeller and I don't
forget

mom and grandma in their see-through rainhats
from Boots drug store
Cindy   at the counter   with I Dream of Jeannie hair
shows them how to wear it   so their hair doesn't get flat
she always calls me doll   sounds like she has marbles in her throat

Dorothy   our upstairs neighbour   our friend
teaches Mama Maryam a shortcut to the community centre

we walk through streaks of rain
that slice frosty wind
too cold to play in puddles
mom pulls me into the moist warmth of her ESL classroom
wall to wall carpeting
today is Multicultural Day
everyone has brought a platter to share

the teachers, Mrs. Jones and Mrs. Parker are there to greet us
*oh, this is Sareh! Nice to see you Sareh! We love your mom and
grandma
they have told us all about you!*

I meet their classmates
 know their names   now their faces   friends
but only at school
people just like us
from all over the world

we feast on dumplings, egg rolls, deviled eggs, Turkish Dolmeh
(tastes different than Mama Maryam's), Samosas, Tamales, and
triangle-shaped ham sandwiches on squishy white bread with
butter, something I crave the rest of my life

oven-baked bread embraces
this cold drizzly grey day
we are not yet accustomed
we are welcome
 we belong

him, New Brunswick, 1983[18]

I

long narrow
chip rock road

                curving, rolling   leading nowhere

fireflies dance with dusk
        air emanates stillness
              silence cloaks nightfall
endless sky   scattered with stars

II

tall narrow clapboard houses, homesteads
        spring along street shoulders

fields forever   on either side

neighbours for generations
together weather life   keep a polite distance
             yet always heed the call for support

III

home warm
smells of beef barley soup and Dad's baked potatoes

---

[18] My husband's life growing up.

after a long day   time spent at the rink
everyone comes in from the cold
hurriedly to sit at the table
 someone turns on CBC
happy dog tails wag   thump on walls

home glows amber
onto white snow
  night falls on the quiet little town

enisled

my grandmother is a seamstress
she sews together pieces of time

my cousin and I sit criss-cross on the carpet
newspaper print, needle, and thread
folds of fabric all around us

family in Berlin, Tehran, Los Angeles, Vancouver, London, New
York, Rome, Dallas, Sydney, San Francisco, Madrid, Seattle,
Vienna, Washington DC, Frankfurt, San Diego

displaced

my grandmother is a seamstress
she sews together enisled stories of loved ones
shaping unseen family
into life

The word "Khaleh" means mother's sister. The word "Ameh" is father's sister. We sometimes also use "Khaleh" for our mother's best friends. To my Khaleh Parvin's consternation, when I was very young, I gave her the nickname "Mamaly", which really stuck. She once told me she had always hoped I would call her Khaleh, but for some reason it felt performative when I tried to use it. I eventually gave-up and thought the reason "Khaleh Parvin" did not work was because it was too ordinary a title for someone so extraordinary.

Khaleh Parvin (Mamaly)

her assured smile
cast in ruby red
left love prints on either side of my face
glowing with glee
my chubby fingers hurriedly searched her purse for compact
mirrors to see
the deep-red-lip stamp of approval

you really should know
her laughter rolled like the deepest bluest sea

and she rocked me in her arms, singing songs of the far east
her voice, a beacon to my soul's return
> gliding on ocean beds
>
> rocking me
>
> her sweet sound waves
>
> rocking me
>
> heart filled with music
>
> rocking me
>
> in rhythm and melody
>
> rocking me
>
> lost in reverie
>
> rocking me
>
> to my centre

cellophane of saffron

I

I hear my name, *Sareh! Saaaaaareh!*

dark forest green
navy black
 surround me

not a sound but my father calling my name
his voice echoing
off trees and mountains
too dark and cold to stay outside (I hadn't noticed)

I pedal back super-fast
through trees pass cul-de-sacs
wheels wheezing
breath billowing
eyes stinging from cold night air

porch light cuts
white light in navy night

I swerve down the driveway into the carpark

inside the warm house
my hands hurt

begin to thaw
red hot cold
bulging and itchy

II

the metronome of life builds a steady gait

I read about the slow movement
I read about mindfulness
I rush through all I am meant to savour

moments flash like neon bulbs
in the corner of my eyes

life is like the 80s music videos
that once confused me
my teeth hurt

today, when I look into Mamaly's eyes
time seems to stand still
love and humour in her gaze
unchanged
hope
unchanged

hope
she should have lost
 could have lost

saved

in the nook of her swiftly packed luggage

held between

cellophanes of saffron and envelopes of old family photos

dad's immigrant song

I

baba,
my weft of life relies on ideals of you
superhero
  as I weave these words
        I tell our tale
        spin our web, to catch your fall

when we got out alive
      you drove unfamiliar streets at night   the best job for an
immigrant

they would never have guessed
you came from an estate home
lined with cars parked between cypress trees
each with its own driver

they sat behind you on black vinyl seats
        judging you   your accent
their smell of liquor seeping the taxi
you laugh, *they are just getting to know us*

when we got out alive
you lost material comforts
not us, your prize

II

too early for you to be awake after driving the nightshift
mom and grandma being quiet in the kitchen
I run into your room (our living room)
climb into your bed (our pullout couch)
you stir and smile and laugh and kiss and we play
because you are my dad
and I am your everything
I know

I race towards the TV, turn the dial
we watch Bob Barker give away prizes
American Dream material wealth shines in our living room
mixed with the smell of homemade bread

solace

solicitude holds me by a string

my grandma sews into my sweater

holding me together

against the diatribes I face at school

    Your dad drives that cab? Does it smell like Indian food, they all smell like Indian food.

    Your lunch looks like dog food, woof woof.

    I can't understand when your parents talk to me, you will have to translate their English.

friends' words grasp me tight

make me feel we belong

    My great grandparents immigrated here too.
    I love your mom's food- let's go to your place.
    My parents say Iran was once really beautiful.
    The only non-immigrants are First Nations.

Dear Sally Field,

Hi, you don't know me but I think of you often. You first came into my life back in 1991; that was a big year. Operation Desert Storm ended, Nirvana released Nevermind, suburban kids were playing *911 Is A Joke* on their radios, I was in grade 7, enjoying what felt like the prime of my life, and your film *Not Without My Daughter* hit the big screen.

Sally, you may not know this, but your movie came out at a time when the image of "crazy Iranians" was finally dissipating from mainstream media. It was a welcome interlude for my family and I. We were able to just be ourselves without feeling like we needed to prove that we were normal, nice people.

Unfortunately, your movie put that barbaric image back in the limelight. An interesting thing happened as a result: a cohesion developed in my culture of origin. Your movie sparked an agreement amongst all Iranians: right-wing, left-wing, extremists, moderates, and liberals. It is no small feat. It rarely happens because we are a divided people, unable to come to much of a consensus on anything, really, but we sure agreed on our dislike for your film, and sadly, for you, dear Sally.

Somehow, you, the leading lady, took the blame. That sucks—I hate that, but at the time, I hated you for taking the role. The problem is that the movie you starred in was a retelling of an old Islamophobic story. Even as a 12-year-old I could see the injustice in portraying Iranian men and society as primitive and abusive to women. Why couldn't you have starred in something addressing the strong matriarchal system in modern Iranian society and the rich archaeological and anthropological evidence of women in power (female mayors, ministers, landowners, and CEOs) dating back as far as ancient Iran, to widen the lens through which North Americans could see true aspects of Iranian society and culture? I suppose that script wasn't written yet.

While it is true that Islamic Fundamentalism is sexist and deeply patriarchal, this is equally true of all fundamentalist religions. Yours could have been a movie that shone the light on a misunderstood culture and revealed the universality of women's struggles in all nations under all major religions.

Sally, I am sure you agree with me on all these points. Luckily, Iranians are a lighthearted people and by the time Mrs. Doubtfire came along, many could not hold onto the grudge against you. I mean, some still do, but many don't. So, now you are back to being just one of the many things Iranians do not agree on.

In ambiguity,
Sareh Farmand

Blood of flowers[19]

prepare
pestle   mortar

petals turn
orange   crimson
onto   silk   wool

       you   far away   from where you began

prepare
pestle   mortar

petals turn
indigo

dyed blue
from our tears

[19] Inspired by <u>Blood of Flowers</u> by Anita Amirrezvani.

what am I to you

another
an other

I am
a victim of Islamic Fundamentalism   yet I am Muslim
this is the dystopian utopia
I call home

when a targeted act of racial violence occurs, I appreciate your call,
the care
but this pain belongs to us all
not just   my *kind*
humankind

I want you to see me as you see yourself
see me, the same way you see all the Sarahs, with an H or without,
with an A or an E

> *(Well…"* my friend's mom said, *"we are surprised. THIS is
> Sarah?"* Yes, this is me. Not another. *"We didn't expect
> to see a Sarah with dark-hair-and-dark-eyes. We were not
> expecting a Sarah that looks like you."* simply said,
> with kindness and humour and warmth. We all laugh.)

I am never what you expect, but I always wish I were
just. like. you.

(Like all the Sarahs in the songs from the 70s. Likely
dancing on roller-skates on Venice Beach— like all the real
Sarahs do. Corn silk-hair, not a care in the world, not an
other.)

We are taught in sacred spaces: we are all one
yet create the Other
rage and attribution feel holy
the Other is to blame
    for everything
    they did not melt enough
    nor try hard enough to sound like us

    (I drift to sleep to echoes of English language tapes,
    my parents practicing pronunciation
    in our orange-brown kitchen.)

all the things I wanted to say when I was 15 or 16 years old

I know I am different.
I know I am different than what you are used to.
I know my family is different. I don't want to draw attention to all
the ways we are unlike you. Please, please, let's just pretend we are
the same. I think deep down inside we are.

Also, please don't ask me to explain my "culture." You really want
me, a kid, to bridge the gap for you? To fill in all the six-o'clock
news missing pieces. Barbara Walters had her chance[20], and blew it,
or maybe she just followed her script: make the Shah look bad.

I'd rather focus on how we are the same. I'd rather tell you about
my dad's favourite food: fish and chips, and my mom's favourite
band: The Beatles. And how in every culture we drink tea.

I don't want to be different, yet I am, and you don't want to ignore
it, because it's your way of being nice and it interests you. It shows
respect. I see that. Thank you. And sometimes I'm okay talking
about it, but mostly right now— I just want to fit in. I want you
to see me as any other kid that walks through your door. One who
does not have a better grasp of international politics and diplomacy
than the others.

---

[20] This is in reference to the 1977 interview which many Iranians felt painted Iran as an underdeveloped nation
and the king of Iran as a tyrannical leader. Many Iranians, however, agreed that the Shah was tyrannical and cite
SAVAK (the National Organization for Security and Intelligence, the special agency of domestic security and
intelligence service of Iran during the reign of the Pahlavi dynasty) as evidence.

Because the thing is, I am not just different from your kid and our friends. I am different from most Iranian kids. It's like I don't fit in a-n-y-w-h-e-r-e. Most of the Iranians at our school just moved here from Iran— they grew up in Iran. I am nothing like them. They don't talk with a Canadian lilt in their Farsi. They don't say "ummm" while searching for a Persian word. They know slang and swears— I only know my parent's Farsi.

I don't know what they see when they see me, but I know they don't see themselves. I am an anomaly to them. The girls stare at my clothes as I walk down the hall. Some of them give me dirty looks, and I don't even know them. I give extra sweet smiles, so they know I am nice. I hear two boys speak in Farsi and point my way, "Look at her, she thinks she's white! HA!" they look at me, confident I didn't understand a word, and I respond: "Fekr kardee![21]"

I am Pierre Trudeau's vision for Multiculturalism. I am a mix-culture-Canadian.

I know that's not the type of Canadian Stephen Harper was referring to when he said, "old stock Canadian". That's just another way of dividing us and he got it wrong. Look around you: this is Canada. We are multicultural, and I am proud to be Canadian.

---

[21] "So you think!" in Farsi.

landed immigrant

> *immigrant*
> *refugee*

my mother's body seizes

subconsciously her shoulders shoot up
broad smile closes
eyebrows pinch

my muscles clench   mom is upset
> *we are not refugees, she says,* her voice a little pitchy
> *we are not immigrants,* her words come out abruptly
> *we are landed immigrants,* she says assuredly

her shoulders drop
broad smile returns
she sits tall
 clearly an important distinction
  but I, the *landed immigrant*, confused about the difference

~ ~

bar is noisy
my hair already smells of cigarette smoke
I order another vodka soda

where are you from, the guy beside me asks

north shore, I say, because I've learned the West Van distinction
paints a picture:
country clubs and massive homes   far from my reality

*oh, no, I mean, where are you from from, like where are your parents
from? ooooh,* great, another distinction that will paint a disparate
image far from my reality so, I try to be precise and say: *Iran, but
not the Iran you know and have learned about from TV; my family
is from pre-revolutionary Iran— like the Iran that was similar to
Canada (but more chic and European than Canada) in the 70s, that
Iran. So, my parents fled when Ayatollah—*

yeah, I thought you were Spanish, I'm really into Spanish music, he
says

--

I visit my friend whose parents were Mujahidin
I never thought I would be friends with a Persian Communist
I cannot tell my aunt about this friend; she will have a fit

his house has none of the Iranian home markings I am used to
seeing
void of a formal living room arranged for conversational ease
 no crystal bowls and silver dishes filled with dried fruits, nuts, and
chocolates
 no Middle Eastern inspired paintings or fake impressionist art on
the walls in heavy frames
 no Persian carpets, not even a Persian runner

his mom greets me, and I am instantly at ease, I don't feel judged
are they really Persian if I don't feel judged by his mom, I wonder
he tells me that his parents also had to flee Iran for political reasons

his parents wanted communism
mine wanted a constitutional monarchy
our parents would not have been friends had they met in Iran
our families both fled to Germany

I lived in a rental apartment
he, a refugee camp

the mall, 1995

we find a way to make it work, you say
we find a way, eventually it all works out, you say it twice to
convince us both
smiling your warm smile   eyes twinkling   cheeks pressing up into
your temples
laugh lines around your eyes crease deep into your skin

this, while you're washing the floors of your pizza parlour at the
mall

you made so much pizza when we were living in Germany, I
remember

so much, you promised you would never eat it again, you say, laughing
you mimic me: *Daddy, man deegeh nemeekhoram pizza!*

nobody in the food court could ever imagine you were part of the
gentry and you don't care
those things don't matter, you taught us

*were you scared when we stayed in Germany, not knowing where we'd
end up?* I ask

*No, I was hopeful, nobody believed the revolution would last. I got
scared when we arrived in Canada. I remember we were waiting for
your uncle to come get us at the airport.*

It was so cold: Vancouver, at dusk, in October. I held your hand in mine, and put my free hand in my pocket, to keep warm. I felt 250 dollars—the only money left to our name.

My daughter, in one hand, and all the money I had to take care of her in the other.

I was scared then.

oh, we're Italian

my older cousins used to pretend they were Italian
it made everyone feel more at ease

unless, you gave off Mafioso vibes
which my cousins definitely did not
(they were the sweet, preppy, tennis player type)
there was nothing to fear in an Italian

Italians have: pasta, *it's amore,* and pious nuns
Iranians have: sour cherries, *hell be to the US* chants, and Khomeini
the creepiest looking leader alongside Sauron and Voldemort

it was safer to say you were Italian
nobody asked:
have you seen Not Without My Daughter?

Sunday morning mourning

bustling, hopeful Old Iran
lives in our parents and grandparents
for decades, they struggle to sustain her within us
preserve her   culture   music   language   poetry
somewhere she must thrive

my mom no longer has to rely on old stories
she emails us YouTube clips, online archival pictures of pre-revolutionary Iran, and her favourite old music videos, and writes:

Sareh Jan, you were not born yet when this was my favourite song, but I loved it so much and had Maman make me mini-jupe to match the same one Googoosh is wearing here.

and

Sareh Jan, you should show Andy and Theresa and Joe[22], so they know Iran looked so beautiful without the pollution and nobody in Hijab.

~ ~

in the 90s, our parents use the burgeoning Iranian TV industry
from LA
to cultivate culture in their North American offspring

our ritual every Sunday at 11am PST

---

[22] My husband and my parents-in-law.

Dad cues the VCR, Mom quickly pours us one last cup of sweet
black tea,
Grandma shoos us to congregate around the television set in the
family room,
attendance is mandatory
even homework isn't a way out

my brother and I are bored straight except for Shohreh Aghdash-
loo's segment
and images of pre-revolutionary Iran set to melancholy music
the mourning piece of the morning

~ ~

in 1994, Houshmand Aghili sets a phrase we hear all the time
"Cheh Khabar Az Iran"
to music: *What news do you have of Iran?*

*What news of people left behind? What's it like in Iran now? Is the
Lady in Red still in Ferdowsi square? Is the nice shop clerk, next to the
high school, still there? What news of the life we mourn every morning?*

safe inside

moments in time swirling inside
glass bottles on shelves
  in my mind

I wander up there
play moments
  find who you were robbed of being

carefree mother, fearless father, aunt who never stopped singing
grandmother never lonesome

        safe inside
glass bottles on shelves in my mind

sound

in Tehran, does the sound build?

      the holy sound:
        allah-o-akbar

does it billow their lungs
(grey from smoke and exhaust fumes)
release with the fluttering wings
of morning birds?

does that only occur in movies
of foreign countries
that seem to get along with the West?

powerful homogenous West
like the popular group
decides which weird kid is cool to talk to
and which one is too weird
banished   isolated
tariffs   sanctions

sanctions cause hungry breast-feeding mothers
cause poverty-stricken fathers to prostitute their daughters, cause
children at midnight to sell flowers and sweet lemons to cars stuck
at red lights

while the mullahs' kids attend private universities abroad
drive Lamborghinis down narrow cobblestone streets lined with
yellow jasmines
(where my mother used to play)
Louis Vuitton veils fluttering in the wind
gangsta rap on the subwoofer
authentic Chanel dangling from chains
sippin' Russian vodka
#untouchables

allah-o-akbar

dis-ease

Patient: X   Gender: Female   Age: 60

Presents as:
Loving and dedicated mother, aunt, sister, daughter, cousin, friend, and teacher. Compassionate sociable empath. Lover of poetry, politics, fashion, and music. Blessed with a melodic voice and perfect pitch.

Diagnosis: frontotemporal dementia or FTD, more specifically primary progressive aphasia or PPA

Symptoms: (not an exhaustive list)
- A slow but progressive loss of vocabulary and ability to understand what people are saying, leading to mutism
- Increased difficulty recognising familiar people or household items
- Increased problems carrying out normal daily living activities
- Increased muscular trouble, similar to Parkinson's disease, such as a tremor
- Increased difficulty using arms and legs

Cause: Forced departure from homeland, fear for safety of self and loved ones because of Ayatollah Khomeini.

Treatment: none.

<u>Patient:</u> Y   <u>Gender:</u> Male   <u>Age:</u> 65

<u>Presents as:</u>
Gregarious, kind, compassionate, empathetic, loyal, and joyful
father, brother, son, son-in-law, uncle, friend, and neighbour.
Impassioned by family, friends, laughter, music, adventure, travel,
knowledge, and nature. Self-taught musician. Perfect pitch.

<u>Diagnosis:</u> early onset Parkinson's and dementia

<u>Symptoms:</u> (not an exhaustive list)
- Apathy
- Confusion
- Muscular tremors
- Impaired posture and balance
- Increased risk of injury due to loss of balance
- Speech changes: speaks softly, slurs, has developed a
  stutter
- Slowed movement (bradykinesia) making simple tasks
  difficult and time consuming
- Shorter gait
- Difficulty getting on and off chairs.
- Drags feet while walking
- Rigid muscles occurring in arms and legs
- Stiff, painful muscles limit range of motion

<u>Cause:</u> Forced departure from homeland, fear for safety of self and
loved ones because of Ayatollah Khomeini.

<u>Treatment:</u> none.

Patient: Z   Gender: Female   Age:29

Presents as energetic, compassionate, empathetic, and loyal teacher, wife, friend, sister, daughter, cousin, and granddaughter. Excitedly nervous to embark on the new journey of motherhood.

Diagnosis: baby blues and postnatal depression

Symptoms: (not an exhaustive list)
- Extreme agitation and anxiety
- No sense of self
- Suicidal thoughts and actions
- Rapid mood swings
- Bizarre behaviour, such as quick to anger and overreact to neutral and benign incidents
- Shows signs of obsessive-compulsive disorder (OCD)
- Inability and refusal to sleep
- Extremely overwhelmed

Cause: Deeply engrained anxiety caused by the forced departure from homeland of loved ones, and fear for safety of loved ones and self, because of Ayatollah Khomeini.

Treatment: none.

lucid[23]

this highway, this road, leads to your old home, I remember so
well, it's surprising
I used to sing, where is my King, long ago, before darkness had
found me

was it silent in the car, we drove near, we drive far, or did we fill it
with many whispers?
I don't recall, details, they all seem so loosely tied together
with silver string, and pretty things, I try so hard to sew them in order
but, the needle, weightless, slips between my fingers

upon my walls, pictures of you all, my life, my love, and my laughter
what was I to you, a child, mother, sister, friend
roles that bind us together

it was not all as it seemed, not nearly what we planned, while play-
ing sticks in sand
but we created a new dream, better than many:
big family dinners we had
late night music parties, and heartaches shared together

within this new space: vast   green and moss   conjure loss
yet their furling forests secure me
clean streams, grey ocean, and
glacial lakes the Canadians tell me

---

[23] In the voice of my mom's sister, Khaleh Parvin, whom I call Mamaly.

what they would not name: the ice in their stares, cold chilling, the
cod they were selling

it'd be impolite, to draw attention to light: false truths, they were
believing
pictures on screens, reflecting a blue-green in their
family-dining-TV-rooms
made false images of us all, the great, the weak, me, and my native
country

VIP

On cabin ski weekends
nobody wants to cross with me.

       questions by border officers
usher to a different lane
broad non-menacing smile on my face
see I am nice
drive our hushed car   slowly   gingerly

Really? Every time? friends whisper in the quiet car
I laugh it off (keep it light)
wave it off
a friend grabs my hand
(moral support)
VIP Lane, my friend jokes, *Very Intelligent Persian Lane*

      same questions by different officer
      as if casual conversation
      led inside
      same questions by this officer
      as if in passing

      you all sit back here while we ask her some questions
      I smile reassuring

      led to front counter

wait

new officer

computer's *just warmin'-up*

same questions

retina scan

wait

new officer

same questions

fingerprints

new officer

this one flirts, *maybe I'll hold you back here just for the night*

laugh it off (keep it light)

same questions

picture taken, *don't smile for this*

I won't.

seamless

I didn't know
  you could love me

your white gaze
  on my brown body

your blue eyes bathe
  deep in black

hot blood beats fast   in cold crisp morning walks   from snowbank
linens
where I leave strands of my ebony hair
sow
  clay prayer tablets
  grains of sand
  obsidian prayer beads
in your palms and feet
while you sleep

integrating you with me, me to you
            I didn't know it could be so seamless

birthday wishes

on the eve of my 40th birthday, I visit my grandmother

I kiss her concave cheeks
feel her thinning skin under my lips
tip of her nose always cold

holds me like she did when I was small
her wrinkled hands   veins like roots
carry us all on her limbs
in her heart, a nest of comfort
love exudes from her amber-brown eyes   envelops me

I sit next to her leaning body, remembering
how I'd curl into the warm spot of her bed
in the morning
when she'd get up to make tea

Tomorrow you turn 40, she says
Yes, and in 3 days you turn 91!
Her eyebrows jump, as if surprised by this fact, and a smile fills her
face, she laughs:
Yes! I am so lucky to have made it this long!
She cocks her head and looks dismayed:
*I did not get you a gift. I have been too sick to go to the mall, what can
I get you?*
Holding back my tears:

You have always given me all of you, what more do I need?
She smiles, *Ghorboonet*[24].

You are turning 40 and you have realized everything I ever wished for you,
so for your 40th birthday I am going to make another kind of wish.

40 years have passed since the Revolution, and I truly thought by now the regime would have crumbled. For your 40th birthday, I wish for freedom in Iran.

That is all I want for my birthday also, she says, looking up toward the sky

---

[24] A term of endearment that translates to I would die for you.

half moons

when I was small
          we caught little bugs with see-through wings   set them free

your hands bigger than mine
comparing half moons set into each of our cuticles

I wished my hands would look like yours   *Do they?*
          your laugh murmurs in my ear   low rumble   under each lobe

your safety, stronger than an angry revolution
carried me
     softly
    safely
    hot feet in cool sea-salt drenched sand

your shoulder
the perfect width, strength
for me to cry on
no matter how old

we rode our bikes in cold forest trails

I know by heart, the lines on the palm of your hands
briefly imperfect by soap-water-induced-eczema
scrubbing pizza pans

> your shoes smelled of
> butter

I was small
now I am big
> and you are gone

thin veil

during carpool, in traffic
        I wonder if you still remember me and our love
        even though I set you free

we gingerly lifted the veil   unaware
cold frost within me
forever without you

the doctors assured me hearing is the last to go
so I whispered
dad,
you were an excellent dad
you always held my hand, and believed in me, always
it breaks me to say, you can go now
I read somewhere if you truly love someone
you set them free, I think this is what they meant

I brought my iPhone and played your favourite songs from the 60s
and 70s
Vigen, Hayedeh, and The Animals' House of the Rising Sun
echoed through the 7th floor of Lions Gate Hospital

no more suffering for you
no more sadness and heartbreak, for you deserve better than a
country that fucked you over
and threw you out

you gave love and laughter in return

in stillness of twilight
between here and thereafter
I hope you have found
belonging

surrogate family

I write a post on Instagram about you today
I am working on the poem "Khaleh Parvin"
my heart is heavy with memories of you I long to relive

I can feel the soft skin of your slim hands in mine
smell your face cream: hints of rose and chamomile
hear your sing-song voice, each intonation

I see you
   sitting on the beige and pink chesterfield in your formal living
room
a broad smile upon your face
   behind the wheel of your brown Chevy hatchback waiting for me
at my school
your hair perfectly coiffed and cherry red lipstick on your heart-
shaped lips
   the last time we walked along the seawall together our arms
linked
we were in complete silence
your eyes and smile said you still knew me
no words needed

I write a post on Instagram about you today
and am flooded with messages from old friends, your old students,
asking about you

the same old friends that moved to Vancouver around the same time we did
sent their kids to you for Farsi lessons, became our surrogate extended family
on the weekends shared in comforting customs of big Persian dinner parties

our little community of people who could rely on one another in ghorbat[25] comfort me today after I write a post on Instagram about you

---

[25] Ghorbat translates to "a foreign place, being a foreigner, or being in a place where one feels like a foreigner".

Sepi

you left without saying goodbye

after the tents built with pillows and bed sheets

after the homemade pizza parties and dancing to our parent's
Persian Pop songs
strolling home under navy skies of Rome, reciting poetry in the
dead of night

after school day morning walks with my cousins on cobblestone to
the International school
my uncle picking up the kids in his second-hand Fiat

after we move to North Vancouver and you braid my hair while I
sit on the floor of your room
we hear our parent's Persian Pop music through the floor
but listen to Billy Idol, Joan Jett, and Duran Duran on your clock
radio

I pretend to read the novels on your bedside table
you braid my hair
after forever and ever I idolize
you

after, I touch your short hair, *what did you do to all your hair! you
cut it so short!*

like brillo
       (cancer? a wig?)
you took any inkling away with your smile

you left without saying goodbye

I

close the door
turn on 90s alternative rock
   don't want to be needed right now

sit on my bed
pick a pink metallic pencil
from its box
slick between my fingers
point sharp
strong

it glides colour onto the white crisp paper
soft scratches
colour between the lines
enter the sacred

I am 40, not 15
        don't want to be needed right now

II

music and motion of colouring take me backward
to my parents' home
my forever family home

safe inside the resin bubble in my mind

west coast post-and-beam
filled with light   ocean views
dream home in Canada
back deck barbeques
          smell of safety under summer stars

next door, a carpenter and his homemaker wife
down the road, a teacher and principal
annual block parties bring everyone together

on hot afternoons
faint sauna smell from the wood panelling fills our home

on cold winter nights, who builds the fire in the woodburning hearth?
dad concedes defeat to Mama Maryam

basmati rice always on the stove
grandma watches Wheel of Fortune while sewing
mom and dad cook and clean together in the kitchen
brother plays basketball in the backyard

III

our home
gutted

new build after new build after infill after infill

drywall new paint and stain and plaster, new

$400 per square foot renos
lumber shortage, so $600 per square foot renos

tree removal bylaws
double lot
perimeter monitoring
stainless-steel
build to the curb
heated garage
heated driveway
heated fake lawn
automatic lights, nobody home

another dimension

Is there a dimension where all the promises my parents made to each other are kept?

Is there a dimension where all their hopes and dreams are realized?

Is there a dimension where the house they built remained their home without bombs raining down?

Is there a dimension where our family flourished?

Is there a dimension where war sirens didn't drown their laughter?

Is there a dimension where I finally bury these thoughts?
Suffocate the ghosts that haunt us.

ego

expand   space   between   thought

          silence

          drops

          on paper

          ink stains turn grey
blurred lines

in (silent space)
compulsion to characterize self   ceases
          pure radiant consciousness survives

Epilogue

the story of humanity
is that of
migration
threaded deep in our consciousness
DNA strands search
belonging

Acknowledgements

Since I was little, I secretly dreamed of being a writer, but I felt it would be an unreliable career choice after my parents left all their stability and worldly comforts to afford me a better life.

But the dream would not let me go. I finally realized everything that my parents did was so that I could be free— free to choose my happiness. This book is a dream come to life because of the support of my family, friends, and colleagues.

Thank you to my ever loving and brave parents, Fariborz Farmand and Nassrin Amirhamzeh, for everything.

Gratitude to my grandmother, Maryam Amirhamzeh, and my Khaleh, Parvin Shahbazi, who taught me the art of storytelling by graciously sharing their stories with us always. Thank you to my brother, Saba Farmand, and my sister-in-law, Catherine Coakley, who always cheer me on. Gratitude to my cousins, Hamed Shahbazi and Hessam Shahbazi, who walked the path of these stories with me and supported me in sharing them; and to all my family, cousins, aunts, and uncles who encouraged me along the way.

Deep gratitude to my darling partner and biggest believer, Andy Donaher, and my children, Lennox and Lachlan. Your strength of character is inspiring. I could not have done this without your confidence in me and in us.

My deep appreciation to my mentors, Betsy Warland and Jonina Kirton, you generously gave your time, knowledge, and experience. You are the midwives to this book and to this new chapter in my life, I am ever grateful to you both. Thank you.

My deep gratitude to my writing family: everyone at SFU's The Writer's Studio 2018, Joanna Baxter for encouraging me to apply in the first place, my poetry cohort (William Brad Akeroyd, Jonathan Bessette, Erin Brown-John, Alex Duncan, Megan J. Frazer, Nadia Grunwell, & Deborah Harford), Jospeh Kakwinokanasum for your extra time and encouragement, my dear writer friends, AKA my Witches-of-WeHo (Koreen Heaver, Dayna Mahannah, & Marnie Mahannah), Dianne Carruthers of the Manifestation Station on Gabriola Island, and Zoë Dagneault for your support and inviting me to meet Ingrid Rose and our Writing from the Body poetry group who gave so generously (Kathryn Alexander, Barbara Baydala, Chris Clancy, Colette Gagnon, Carol Groumoutis, Carole Harmon, John Swanson, & Eljean Wilson).

I would like to acknowledge my friends, near and far, who pushed me to follow my dreams, including my childhood friend, Naz Deravian, for her thoughtful introduction to my amazing substantive editor, Sophie Yendole— your care and creative acumen gave me the greatest courage to push myself as an artist, I am forever grateful. Thank you to my awesome publisher, Matt Joudrey, and all the amazing people at my publishing house, At Bay Press, for their caring form of professionalism. Thank you to my brilliant cover artist, Nazli Ataeeyeh, your heart and talent have me awestruck.

The pre-revolutionary Iranian national anthem starts with, "Ey Iran, Ey marzeh por gohar," which my mom proudly told me meant "Oh, Iran, your borders full of ink" in acknowledgment of all the great Iranian poets. I acknowledge and express gratitude to the many great Iranian poets, writers, artists, and freedom fighters. And last, but not least, my deep gratitude to Canada and the Indigenous lands upon which I have been raised, live, and write. I acknowledge the many stories that are yet to be heard.

The author as a child with her mother and father in Rome after the fall of Iran. Photo: Author's family collection

Photo: Kyrani Kanavaros

Sareh Farmand was born in Tehran at the start of the Islamic Revolution, and grew up in Vancouver, BC. Her first book of poems, *Pistachios in my Pocket*, follows a narrative arc that tells the story of her family's escape from Iran and their experiences as first wave Iranian immigrants to Canada.

She holds degrees in International Relations and Education from UBC and is a 2018 graduate of SFU's The Writing Studio.

She lives in Vancouver, BC with her husband, two sons, and their cat.

Photo: Negin Ataeeyeh

Nazli Ataeeyeh is an Iranian-Canadian visual storyteller, illustrator, and art educator. She was born during the Iran-Iraq War and lived through the oppression of the Islamic dictatorship. Her love for art and children blossomed while volunteering at orphanages in Iran. Nazli continued her passion for art into University where she completed her Masters of Fine Arts in 2011.

After the violent suppression of the youth during the Green Revolution in Iran she decided to immigrate to Canada, landing in Toronto in 2013.

She now lives in Vancouver with her life partner and her rainbow baby, Elio. She teaches art and illustrates books in between baby naps and diaper changes.

Thanks for purchasing this book and for supporting authors and artists. As a token of gratitude, please scan the QR code for exclusive content from this title.